A GUIDE TO
Chinese
Horoscopes

A GUIDE TO
Chinese
Horoscopes

Key concepts
in Chinese astrology

D J BURNS

BARNES
&NOBLE
BOOKS
NEW YORK

Contents

Introduction

How to Use this Book

This book introduces you to the enchanting, ancient world of Chinese astrology. It is a simple guide to Chinese horoscopes, for those interested in understanding its structure and origins. This book makes it easy to use this system of character analysis.

There are numerous tables, illustrations and examples throughout to help you use the information provided. The five sections outlined in this book will give you an introduction to the basic structure of Chinese astrology:

1. An overview of Chinese astrology, taking you back to its origins in the time of Buddha and describing the myths that have survived to the present day.
2. An exploration of the twelve animal signs, providing you with a clear, detailed character profile for each one.
3. Some other key concepts of Chinese astrology which will enhance your general understanding of the system.
4. An explanation of the different "types" of each animal, personalized further by exploring the influence of nature's elements: wood, fire, earth, metal and water.
5. To consolidate, some key techniques for interpreting each animal sign in terms of potential relationships, romance and everyday life.

About Chinese Astrology

Chinese astrology is tied to the customs and beliefs that existed many centuries ago in China. Back then, relationships with others — whether for work, intimacy or friendship — were assessed by a wise and esteemed astrologer who would look at dates and times of birth and examine the influences of the ruling animals and elements for those dates and times. These factors were used for making predictions about the relationship's strengths, weaknesses and overall success.

This book will help you to:

- Prepare your own astrological profile and that of others, and interpret their meanings.
- Identify strengths and weaknesses in a given profile, and learn how to work with them.
- Compare profiles and identify areas of compatibility and/or conflict.
- Make more appropriate choices in all areas of life, from your career to friends and relationships.

In general, this book will help you to gain a more informed understanding of who you are and how you relate to others and their environments. You will also come to appreciate the rich uniqueness of each individual and his or her particular strengths and weaknesses, and you will learn how the differences between individuals can complement and support each other.

The Age of Buddha

The great Buddha is said to have lived around the years 563–483 BC. This was a time when myths, legends and tradition were considered important aspects of daily life.

Legend says that, when the great Buddha found enlightenment and was ready to leave the Earth, he invited all the land's creatures to his kingdom to say farewell before his departure. Only twelve animals arrived, in this order: the rat, the ox, the tiger, the hare, the dragon, the snake, the horse, the sheep, the monkey, the rooster, the dog and finally the pig.

To thank the animals for answering his call, Buddha decided to celebrate each of them. Their reward was that each new year would be celebrated in their honor.

Accordingly, in every twelve-year cycle, each of the twelve animals is celebrated in turn. This means that people born during a specific year will be influenced, in terms of personality and life events, by the animal which that year celebrates. This book describes what these influences are, and how they can affect your life.

The Animal Signs

Signs for the Year, Month and Time of Birth

Each of the twelve animals of Chinese astrology has distinct personality traits associated with it. These traits are said to be transferred to those born in the year governed by that animal. This is your dominant sign.

Ruling year of birth = Dominant sign

The traits of the animal sign governing your year of birth will describe your personality. This is the personality that others see — the one you show to the world. However, this can be moderated by the traits of the animals ruling over your month and time of birth. Combining the three elements will result in a detailed, unique character profile for each person (see the List of Years and Astrology Signs on page 78).

Ruling month of birth = Love sign

The traits of the animal sign governing your month of birth will reveal your character in intimate relationships. Knowing these traits will help you create a more detailed profile, which will enable you to seek a compatible partner in any intimate situation.

Key Personality Traits

Animal	Ruling month	Ruling time of birth	Key traits
1. Rat	December	11pm–1am	Ambition, intelligence
2. Ox	January	1am–3am	Tenacity, patience
3. Tiger	February	3am–5am	Courage, dominance
4. Hare	March	5am–7am	Flexibility, balance
5. Dragon	April	7am–9am	Power, dynamism
6. Snake	May	9am–11am	Wisdom, influence
7. Horse	June	11am–1pm	Vitality, agility
8. Sheep	July	1pm–3pm	Serenity, peace
9. Monkey	August	3pm–5pm	Wittiness, cleverness
10. Rooster	September	5pm–7pm	Alertness, honorableness
11. Dog	October	7pm–9pm	Justice, loyalty
12. Pig	November	9pm–11pm	Carefreeness, contentedness

Ruling time of birth = Ascendant sign

The animal sign ruling over the time of your birth is your ascendant sign. The personality traits associated with your ascendant animal sign serve to modify and further specify the personality structure determined by the animal ruling over your year of birth.

Ruling Direction and Season

Chinese astrology embraces a broad range of factors, such as space and direction, and the seasons, which embody the continual cycle of nature. Hence each animal in the Chinese zodiac is also said to rule over a direction (east, west etc.) and a particular season. These factors can help you to understand each animal profile from a broader perspective, but are not essential for uncovering the core personality.

For Example

If you were born on 27th March, 1966 at 7pm, your dominant animal sign (based on the year of your birth) is the Horse, your love sign (based on the month of your birth) is the Hare and your ascendant sign (based on the time of your birth) is the Dog. By combining the traits of these three animal signs you will be able to determine your unique character profile.

The Chinese Lunar Calendar

Unlike the Western system, which records time in solar years — a solar year is the Earth's 365-day rotation around the sun — the Chinese system measures time in lunar years, which follow the moon's orbit around the Earth. The Chinese new year falls on a different date every year, either in January or in February. If you were born during these months, consult the List of Years and Astrology Signs to find out which animal and element dominates the year you were born in.

Character Profiles of the Animals

In the section that follows, there is a detailed character profile for each of the twelve animals. In the chapters "Interpreting Chinese Astrology" and "Meeting your Match", you will see how certain personality traits can be revealed in specific situations.

The Ambitious, Intelligent Rat

Rats are the resourceful masterminds of the Chinese zodiac. Highly communicative and endowed with abundant intelligence and financial acumen, they are driven by the desire to accumulate wealth to ensure their financial security.

Their superior analytical skills guarantee them career success. They make excellent strategic partners in business, where they are motivated just as much by accolades as they are by financial reward.

Being social creatures, Rats are at home in groups. They love to entertain, and maintain active social diaries. They are perceived by their friends as both tasteful and elegant, in an understated fashion. Given sufficient praise and applause from loved ones, Rats make loyal, protective and committed partners and family members.

The Rat ascendant: For those born between 11pm and 1am
The Rat as the ascendant sign stimulates the mental aspects of the personality, and boosts both social charms and communication skills.

Rats at their best
Intelligent, accomplished, charming, innovative, loyal, empathetic, ambitious

Rats at their worst
Secretive, anxious, calculating, possessive, stingy, excessive, neurotic, critical, egotistical

Energy ~ Yang
Element ~ Water
Time ~ 11pm–1am
Month ~ December
Direction ~ North
Season ~ Winter

The Tenacious, Patient Ox

Oxen are direct, principled and dedicated people who like to tread the well-worn paths of tradition and respectability. They are trustworthy and grounded; when they give you their word, they will not let you down. Their core talent is their enormous reserve of physical energy, which they can skillfully harness and manage over long periods of time.

Apart from their physical strength, Oxen are also endowed with a keen appreciation of beauty. They will often give in to their need to indulge their senses.

The Ox ascendant: For those born between 1am and 3am
The Ox as the ascendant sign adds practicality, determination and physical energy to the personality, as well as an appreciation of sensual pleasures.

Oxen at their best
Responsible, hardy, sensible, dutiful, eloquent, industrious, persevering, diligent

Oxen at their worst
Authoritative, stubborn, biased, intolerant, conservative, complacent, depressive, proud

Energy ~ Yin
Element ~ Earth
Time ~ 1am–3am
Month ~ January
Direction ~ North/Northeast
Season ~ Late Winter

The Courageous, Dominant Tiger

In China, the Tiger is the king of the beasts. Those born under this sign have a magnetic, uplifting, motivating presence, and many of the qualities of a good leader.

Tiger people are born adventurers and optimistic daredevils. Full of excited expectation, they know only two speeds: full speed or ground to a halt. They live for the moment, engaging in life passionately and with childlike excitement.

Generally lucky, most Tigers are able to triumph over all types of misadventure — which is important, as they tend to lead volatile lives. Tigers are freedom lovers and rule breakers. They demand plenty of space in their relationships, and as few rules as possible in their daily lives.

The Tiger ascendant: For those born between 3am and 5am

The Tiger as the ascendant sign will endow the personality with passion, courage and conviction. Those with the Tiger sign as the ascendant will also find hidden strengths within themselves when coping with loss or ill health.

Tigers at their best

Brave, giving, charming, idealistic, bold, optimistic, passionate, independent

Tigers at their worst

Reckless, impatient, disobedient, hot-headed, predatory, rebellious, aggressive, overly emotional

Energy ~ Yang
Element ~ Wood
Time ~ 3am–5am
Month ~ February
Direction ~ East/Northeast
Season ~ Early Spring

The Flexible, Balanced Hare

Hares are the intuitive diplomats of Chinese astrology. Blessed with natural style and good taste, they devote many of their resources to their attire and household goods. A secure and harmonious environment is vital for the sensitive Hare.

Hares like to operate in the background, preferring to observe and reflect rather than being actively engaged. They will tactfully handle any issue that arises, and will effortlessly manage disputes, generally achieving peaceful resolutions. They make able negotiators, and have advanced networking skills.

The Hare ascendant: For those born between 5am and 7am
The Hare as the ascendant sign will add flexibility and balance to the personality. Hare ascendants are peace lovers and tactful when dealing with others.

Hares at their best
Discreet, peaceful, perceptive, contemplative, refined, diplomatic, stylish, temperate

Hares at their worst
Indecisive, snobbish, self-indulgent, secretive, self-focused, condescending, moody, detached, conservative

Energy ~ Yin
Element ~ Wood
Time ~ 5am–7am
Month ~ March
Direction ~ East
Season ~ Spring

The Powerful, Dynamic Dragon

As the only mythical creature in the Chinese zodiac, the Dragon inspires wonder, excitement and admiration. Dragons are colorful, confident and vibrant in personality, and win the attention and support of others with great ease.

Dragons like to participate actively in life, engaging their hearts and minds fully with everything that seizes their interest. However, they are free spirits, and will move swiftly on to anything that seems more enticing. Blessed with good luck, great reserves of energy, and optimism, Dragons are skilled at leading, taking on projects few others would be prepared to undertake.

The Dragon ascendant: For those born between 7am and 9am

When the Dragon is the ascendant sign, its influence will create a magnetic personality. Those with a Dragon ascendant usually display independence and confidence.

Dragons at their best

Visionary, passionate, motivated, optimistic, principled, energetic, compelling, vibrant, dynamic

Dragons at their worst

Demanding, dissatisfied, excessive, opinionated, intolerant, overpowering, abrupt, egocentric, unpredictable

Energy ~ Yang
Element ~ Earth
Time ~ 7am–9am
Month ~ April
Direction ~ East/Southeast
Season ~ Late Spring

The Wise, Influential Snake

In China, snakes are admired for their beauty and wisdom. Snake people have a serene presence, and rarely reveal feelings of agitation or stress. Self-disciplined and tradition-loving, they are thinkers rather than doers.

Given their perceptive minds, natural sophistication and reflective natures, Snakes are often sought after for their opinions and counsel. They make skilled negotiators, and will swiftly distinguish themselves in any position of influence.

The Snake ascendant: For those born between 9am and 11am
Having the Snake as the ascendant sign gives rise to reflection on the self, objectivity and wisdom. Snakes radiate sexuality and attractiveness.

Snakes at their best
Discreet, enticing, intelligent, wise, enigmatic, refined, sensual, instinctive, methodical, shrewd, perceptive

Snakes at their worst
Calculating, vengeful, lazy, suspicious, jealous, extravagant, standoffish, possessive, fickle

Energy ~ Yin
Element ~ Fire
Time ~ 9am–11am
Month ~ May
Direction ~ South/Southeast
Season ~ Early Summer

The Vital, Agile Horse

Horses are the restless adventurers of the Chinese zodiac. Energetic and active, they are constantly on the move. They take up causes eagerly and impetuously. They like to live independent lives and to be free to roam and explore all areas of life. They are afraid of being trapped in any situation, and want to live without having to commit themselves long-term to any person, object or goal.

Optimistic, upbeat and energetic, Horses are keenly sought after as friends and personal coaches. They love to socialize and to be the focus of attention. They often maintain their good health and youthful appearance far longer than others.

The Horse ascendant: For those born between 11am and 1pm
The Horse as the ascendant sign adds vitality and physical
agility to the personality. Those with Horse ascendants can also become restless
and bored easily.

Horses at their best
Independent, deft, enthusiastic, youthful, frank, gregarious, enterprising,
energetic, generous, chatty, brave

Horses at their worst
Temperamental, impatient, hot-tempered, irresponsible,
opportunistic, unscrupulous

Energy ~ Yang
Element ~ Fire
Time ~ 11am–1pm
Month ~ June
Direction ~ South
Season ~ Summer

The Serene, Peaceful Sheep

Sheep are the peacemakers of the Chinese zodiac. Calm by nature, they are pacifists, and will recoil from any confrontation. They are also quiet, friendly, patient and extremely adaptable, and get along with others very easily. They make good listeners and are sympathetic friends.

Highly principled, sensitive and artistically talented, Sheep will often find their calling in the fields of music, literature or art. Here they revel in being left alone, free of the influence of others, to express their imagination.

The Sheep ascendant: For those born between 1pm and 3pm
Having the Sheep as the ascendant sign will add peace and serenity to the personality. People with this ascendant sign may be flexible and light-hearted.

Sheep at their best
Adaptable, considerate, compassionate, creative, easy-going, gentle, sincere, careful

Sheep at their worst
Eccentric, vulnerable, sensitive, pessimistic, naive, gullible, self-indulgent, irresponsible

Energy ~ Yin
Element ~ Earth
Time ~ 1pm–3pm
Month ~ July
Direction ~ South/Southwest
Season ~ Late Summer

The Witty, Clever Monkey

Monkeys are renowned for their keen intellects and lively, comic personalities. No challenge is too great for these motivated, ingenious intellectuals. Give a problem to a Monkey and you will be presented with a solution and a plan of action before others have even started on the job.

Monkeys detest routine, and get bored easily with the status quo. They like to test the boundaries in every possible situation.

Monkeys like change; they take risks and can live their lives quite differently from most other people. Their principle is to break the rules, live for the moment, and above all, have fun. Monkeys rarely show their serious side; if they do, they are probably either acting or joking. Their excitement, optimism and daredevil approach to life are irrepressible, and they make a distinct impression on everyone they meet.

The Monkey ascendant: For those born between 3pm and 5pm
The Monkey as the ascendant sign will add mental agility to the personality. Monkeys may also have a keen wit and be skilled at comedy.

Monkeys at their best
Confident, funny, inventive, clever, vibrant, motivating, sociable, sexual, versatile

Monkeys at their worst
Risky, restless, manipulative, immature, deceitful, mischievous, unpredictable, fickle

Energy ~ Yang
Element ~ Metal
Time ~ 3pm–5pm
Month ~ August
Direction ~ West/Southwest
Season ~ Early Autumn

The Alert, Honorable Rooster

Roosters are spirited, fearless, proud individuals who speak their minds and are meticulous in their dress. They are flashy, jumping at every opportunity to socialize and entertain. Desiring the limelight, they love being center-stage.

As they are so keen on appearances, Roosters can be overly sensitive to the criticism of others. Underneath all the bright feathers, they are extremely intelligent. Blessed with acute perception and a yearning for knowledge, they are scrupulous in their attention to detail, and have extraordinarily high standards. A Rooster's life is anything but dull.

The Rooster ascendant: For those born between 5pm and 7pm
The Rooster as the ascendant sign ensures integrity and a sense
of honor. Those with the Rooster as their ascendant are
keenly alert, and quick to voice their opinions.

Roosters at their best
Alert, cultivated, direct, entertaining, expressive, knowledgeable,
meticulous, resourceful, resilient

Roosters at their worst
Vulnerable, critical, proud, frank, argumentative, impulsive, vain,
selfish, pretentious

Energy ~ Yin
Element ~ Metal
Time ~ 5pm–7pm
Month ~ September
Direction ~ West
Season ~ Autumn

The Just, Loyal Dog

Dogs are loyal, principled and just, the humanitarians and protectors of the Chinese zodiac. They live according to a strong code of ethics, and are usually greatly admired and appreciated by others.

Dogs take life seriously. They are perpetually pursuing their compulsion to address the injustices of the world, and they will follow this path even if it means they have to sacrifice their own needs and desires.

Patient and watchful, Dogs operate by instinct, and will choose the right time to act rather than rushing into something unknown. Provided that Dogs have a cause to stand for, they will not be overwhelmed by the pessimism to which they are prone.

The Dog ascendant: For those born between 7pm and 9pm

This ascendant sign will impart an ethical, principled nature. Those with the Dog as the ascendant sign are loyal and just in their dealings with others.

Dogs at their best

Concerned, compassionate, driven, loyal, principled, protective, responsible, idealistic, trustworthy

Dogs at their worst

Anxious, pessimistic, judgmental, distrustful, discouraging, cynical, introverted

Energy ~ Yang
Element ~ Earth
Time ~ 7pm–9pm
Month ~ October
Direction ~ West/Northwest
Season ~ Late Autumn

The Carefree, Contented Pig

Pigs are calm and contented. Stress-free and peace-loving, they are the easiest people to get along with. They like to take life as it comes, focusing on the moment and indulging in everything that delights them. They tend not to set too many goals for themselves, and apply effort only if it will reduce their daily chores instead of increasing them.

Calm, friendly and fun to be with, Pigs are undemanding. However, they do like an opulent life, and would prefer this to be provided by someone else. They know how to enjoy life to the full, and happiness is their most constant emotional state.

The Pig ascendant: For those born between 9pm and 11pm
Having the Pig as the ascendant sign means a carefree attitude to life, and a focus on enjoyment and self-indulgence.

Pigs at their best
Enthusiastic, generous, outgoing, merry, positive, sensual, warm-hearted

Pigs at their worst
Self-indulgent, hot-tempered, excessive, spendthrift, gullible, debauched, naive, materialistic

Energy ~ Yin
Element ~ Water
Time ~ 9pm–11pm
Month ~ November
Direction ~ North/Northwest
Season ~ Early Winter

Key Concepts

The Life Force: Yin/Yang Energy

The basis of Chinese astrology is the concept of energy, or "qi." The Chinese believe that all matter on earth — living creatures and empty space alike — is comprised of "qi," which takes one of two forms, yang or yin. Yang energy is "masculine" or positive energy, and is manifested as extroversion in the personality. Yin energy, in contrast, is "feminine" or negative energy, and is manifested as introversion in the personality. The two forms of energy are opposites, but they are interdependent. For example, while death is a form of yang energy, life is the opposite: yin.

Each of the twelve animals in Chinese astrology exhibits either yang or yin energy. These provide an initial basis for differentiating between the animals, and for determining their potential compatibility or conflict with others.

Yang energy
Rat ~ Tiger ~ Horse ~ Dragon ~ Monkey ~ Dog

Yin energy
Ox ~ Hare ~ Snake ~ Sheep ~ Rooster ~ Pig

The Five Elements

In Chinese philosophy, life is said to revolve around the natural interaction of five elements — wood, fire, earth, metal and water. Just like each of the twelve animals of the Chinese zodiac, each element is associated with specific character traits. Depending on which elements are present on a given date and time, the interaction and overall effect on the personality will be either energizing or stifling.

The first table opposite shows the governing elements, together with the ruling seasons and compass directions (see also page 9). The second table gives both forms of the element cycle — the energizing and the stifling.

Each animal sign has a natural element that influences its core traits. In addition

Element	Attributes	Season	Direction
Wood	Resourceful, dependable, expansive	Spring	East
Fire	Vibrant, passionate, decisive	Summer	South
Earth	Grounded, balanced, patient	Summer's end	Center
Metal	Tenacious, determined, resilient	Autumn	West
Water	Sensitive, communicative, intuitive	Winter	North

Type of cycle	Element order	Effects of order on elements
The energizing cycle	Wood → Fire → Earth → Metal → Water, which in turn energizes Wood, and so on.	Wood is most conducive and best utilised when combined with Fire and/or Water
The stifling cycle	Wood → Earth → Water → Fire → Metal, which in turn stifles Wood, and so on.	Wood is likely to be tempered and underutilised when combined with Earth and/or Metal.

to this, each animal is also influenced by a dominant element, which is determined by the year of birth. This combination of two elements with each animal produces five different personality types for each animal sign. See pages 36–47 for a description of the different animal sign and element combinations.

The Chinese Life Cycle

The Chinese view time as occurring in 60-year life cycles. They believe that a full life is lived over a 60-year period. Hence the 60th birthday is widely celebrated in China, as it is seen as the point at which wisdom is achieved.

A further cycle significant in Chinese philosophy is the one that encompasses the birth of each of the twelve animals, multiplied by the five element signs. It is only once in a 60-year cycle that each of the twelve animal signs occurs in the same year as each of the five element signs (see the List of Years and Astrology Signs). For example, Water Rats were born in the lunar years of 1912 and 1972 — a span of sixty years. As you will see in the List of Years, the year 1984 marks the beginning of the current Chinese life cycle — the 78th.

Animal Sign and Element Combinations

The Dominant Element

In addition to the natural element associated with each animal, there is also an element dominating each lunar year of birth. The element governing the year of birth is the dominant element, and it has a significant influence on the personality.

The dominant element's influence on each animal results in five distinct personality types for each animal. Hence there is, in Chinese astrology, the potential for 60 (12 animals x 5 elements) identifiable personalities. For example, a Water Tiger would be much more easy-going and temperate than its Metal Tiger sibling, who could be quite fiery and volatile.

Check out your animal sign and element combination in this section for a more specific definition of your personality.

The Elements Governing Years of Birth

METAL
See pages 38–39
1900, 1901, 1910, 1911, 1920, 1921, 1930, 1931, 1940, 1941, 1950, 1951,
1960, 1961, 1970, 1971, 1980, 1981, 1990, 1991, 2000, 2001, 2010, 2011

WATER
See pages 40–41
1902, 1903, 1912, 1913, 1922, 1923, 1932, 1933, 1942, 1943, 1952, 1953,
1962, 1963, 1972, 1973, 1982, 1983, 1992, 1993, 2002, 2003, 2012, 2013

WOOD
See pages 42–43
1904, 1905, 1914, 1915, 1924, 1925, 1934, 1935, 1944, 1945, 1954, 1955,
1964, 1965, 1974, 1975, 1984, 1985, 1994, 1995, 2004, 2005, 2014, 2015

FIRE
See pages 44–45
1916, 1917, 1926, 1927, 1936, 1937, 1946, 1947, 1956, 1957, 1966, 1967,
1976, 1977, 1986, 1987, 1996, 1997, 2006, 2007, 2016, 2017

EARTH
See pages 46–47
1918, 1919, 1928, 1929, 1938, 1939, 1948, 1949, 1958, 1959, 1968, 1969,
1978, 1979, 1988, 1989, 1998, 1999, 2008, 2009, 2018, 2019

Born in a Metal Year

1920, 1921, 1930, 1931, 1940, 1941, 1950, 1951, 1960, 1961, 1970, 1971, 1980, 1981, 1990, 1991, 2000, 2001, 2010, 2011

Tenacity, determination, resilience, and physical strength.

THE METAL RAT ~ From Metal comes Water: Strength & structure
Metal gives this Rat mental and physical strength. Metal Rats have strong opinions and need to voice them often. This can make them appear stubborn and inflexible; however, they balance this with supreme efficiency. **Years of birth: 1900, 1960**

THE METAL OX ~ From Earth comes Metal: Engaging & activating
Metal adds even more physical strength and mental willpower to the Oxen. Metal Oxen know exactly what they want, and do not waste time. Not usually affectionate by nature, they make up for this by being reliable providers. **Years of birth: 1901, 1961**

THE METAL TIGER ~ Wood is controlled by Metal: Strength & domination
Metal Tigers are extremely passionate and volatile, and occasionally overbearing. Loaded with confidence and energy, they are usually quite ambitious and ruthless in business dealings. They demonstrate little of the Tiger's usual easy rapport with others. **Years of birth: 1950, 2010**

THE METAL HARE ~ Wood is controlled by Metal: Strength & domination
Metal fills a gap, making up for the Hare's usual lack of perseverance and bravery. Metal Hares are likely to be detached from their emotions when making decisions. They are cunning and manipulative in business affairs. **Years of birth: 1951, 2011**

THE METAL DRAGON ~ From Earth comes Metal: Engaging & activating
The metal element intensifies the Dragon's magnetic and strong-willed personality. With an abundance of confidence and self-appreciation, Metal Dragons do not easily accept defeat or failure. **Years of birth: 1940, 2000**

THE METAL SNAKE ~ Metal is moulded by Fire: Skilful
Metal Snakes are too calculating and discriminating for their own good. They want the best life can offer and will set out with cool logic and detachment to find a position of influence and power. **Years of birth: 1941, 2001**

THE METAL HORSE ~ Metal is moulded by Fire: Energising
Metal Horses are always on the go. Headstrong and hard to tame, they find it impossible to adapt to routine. Metal Horses are addicted to freedom, open spaces and constant change. Their boldness and engaging personalities add to their sexual appeal. When focused, they can be quite productive. **Years of birth: 1930, 1990**

THE METAL SHEEP ~ From Earth comes Metal: Engaging & activating
Metal Sheep have stronger characters than other sheep. They are able to adjust their sensitivities to gain more of what they want from others. Once sure of their foundations, they will embark on a quest for beauty. **Years of birth: 1931, 1991**

THE METAL MONKEY ~ Double Metal: Intellectual pursuits
Double Metal makes these Monkeys intellectually and physically superior to other Monkey types. They rarely rely on others for assistance. They respect money, and will rarely take uncalculated risks with it. In social settings they appear lively, witty, passionate and convincing. **Years of birth: 1920, 1980**

THE METAL ROOSTER ~ Double Metal: Intellectual rigor
Double metal makes these Roosters extremely industrious. They are passionate about their careers and demonstrate a flair for investigation, practicality and detailed decision-making. They can be uncomprising when dealing with others, expecting excellence. **Years of birth: 1921, 1981**

THE METAL DOG ~ From Earth comes Metal: Engaging and activating
Metal Dogs are stern idealists. They are serious and directed individuals, particularly when it comes to questions of morality and justice. Metal Dogs often devote themselves to worthy causes. **Years of birth: 1910, 1970**

THE METAL PIG ~ From Metal comes Water: Strength & structure
Metal Pigs have big appetites for all the pleasures in life. Unlike other Pigs, they work hard to acquire their wants. Extroverted, affectionate and openly demonstrative, Metal Pigs appeal to the opposite sex and can successfully balance their lives between work, fun and love. **Years of birth: 1911, 1971**

Born in a Water Year

1912, 1913, 1922, 1923, 1932, 1933, 1942, 1943, 1952, 1953, 1962, 1963, 1972,
1973, 1982, 1983, 1992, 1993, 2002, 2003, 2012, 2013

Sensitivity, communication skills, intuition, and creativity.

THE WATER RAT ~ Double Water: Intuition, communication & emotions
Double Water lends these Rats a natural eloquence, leading them into communication-centered careers such as public speaking or professional writing. **Years of birth: 1912, 1972**

THE WATER OX ~ Water controlled by Earth: Emotional accessibility
Just what Oxen need — access to their emotional side. Water Oxen are softer and more approachable than other Oxen. Empathetic and considerate, they are still sufficiently practical. **Years of birth: 1913, 1973**

THE WATER TIGER ~ From Water grows Wood: An enhancing combination
Water makes Tigers quiter and more carefree. Water Tigers are highly intuitive. Socially, they have an extroverted, optimistic presence. Water Tigers are sensitive to others' needs. **Years of birth: 1902, 1962**

THE WATER HARE ~ From Water grows Wood: An enhancing combination
Water Hares are supersensitive, acutely aware of themselves in all environments. This can create a neurotic, inwardly focused personality. **Years of birth: 1903, 1963**

THE WATER DRAGON ~ Water is directed by Earth: Empathy & intuition
Dragons need a dose of water to soften their exuberant personalities and occasionally shift their focus from themselves. Water Dragons are far more considerate and caring than other Dragons. **Years of birth: 1952, 2012**

THE WATER SNAKE ~ Fire is controlled by Water: Clarity & intuition
Water Snakes are amazingly gifted — the embodiment of intuitive perception. With their keen sensory acuity, little passes them by. Water Snakes are often found in "spiritual" professions, where they can utilize their gifts to see beyod the obvious. **Years of birth: 1953, 2013**

THE WATER HORSE ~ Fire is controlled by Water: Intuition & mental creativity
Water Horses have less focus on their physical world and have access to natural creative and/or communicative skills. They are often gifted orators, able to build a story to an emotional finale. **Years of birth: 1942, 2002**

THE WATER SHEEP ~ Water is controlled by Earth: Emotions & intuition
Water Sheep engage with life emotionally, rarely using logic or reflection for objectivity. They are easily wounded by criticism and extremely sensitive to their surroundings, and their mental and physical health is accordingly delicate .
Years of birth: 1943, 2003

THE WATER MONKEY ~ From Metal comes Water: Empathy & reflection
Water ensures that these Monkeys are not too quick to trifle with others' feelings. Water Monkeys demonstrate empathy, and will use their keen intellects to solve problems rather than create them. They are more group-oriented than individually motivated. **Years of birth: 1932, 1992**

THE WATER ROOSTER ~ From Metal comes Water: Empathy and intuition
Water Roosters are softer and more flexible than other Roosters. They use their intuition to avoid being too direct with others. With their appealing combination of self-awareness, flamboyance and understanding of others, they are naturally the focus of attention. **Years of birth: 1933, 1993**

THE WATER DOG ~ From Metal comes Water: Empathy
Water Dogs are more reflective and adaptable than other Dogs. They are more lenient on themselves and others, and will allow for much fun and frivolity in their lives. They will also fall for any sad-luck story. Water Dogs are popular with others, and will never want for love, friendship or support.
Years of birth: 1922, 1982

THE WATER PIG ~ Double Water: Intuition, communication & emotions
Double water intensifies the Pig's already emotionally charged personality, making Water Pigs supersensitive to others and overly indulgent. Increasingly introspective with age and experience, Water Pigs' ability to deal with hardships in life can quickly diminish. They will often need the help of others in order to escape their plight. **Years of birth: 1923, 1983**

Born in a Wood Year

1914, 1915, 1924, 1925, 1934, 1935, 1944, 1945, 1954, 1955, 1964, 1965, 1974, 1975, 1984, 1985, 1994, 1995, 2004, 2005, 2014, 2015

Resourcefulness, creativity, spiritual growth, and optimism.

THE WOOD RAT ~ From Water grows Wood: An enhancing combination
Wood Rats display more creative talent and interest in spirituality than other Rats. Their optimism and heightened resourcefulness overcome much of the Rat's usual worries about security, and this frees them to indulge a little in their passions. Caring and empathetic, Wood Rats are popular. **Years of birth: 1924, 1984**

THE WOOD OX ~ Earth is controlled by Wood: Harnessed strengths
Wood Oxen are dependable and stable, clear of purpose and rigid adherents of their principles and values. Highly ethical, they avoid the lightweight and light-hearted. They tend to follow a traditional path, enjoying the comfort and security of a home and family. **Years of birth: 1925, 1985**

THE WOOD TIGER ~ Double Wood: Expansion & personal growth
Double Wood gives the Tiger twice as much gaiety and childlike enthusiasm. Wood Tigers are irrepressible, and will often be surrounded by an adoring crowd. They detest commitment in all forms, preferring to spend their time traveling, exploring, learning and generally experiencing all that life has to offer. **Years of birth: 1914, 1974**

THE WOOD HARE ~ Double Wood: Expansion & personal growth
Wood Hares are usually artistically talented, and have creative occupations. They are quite generous and give freely of themselves. While eager for financial wealth, they are quick spenders, particularly when it comes to traveling for inspiration.
Years of birth: 1915, 1975

THE WOOD DRAGON ~ Earth is utilized by Wood: Harnessed strengths.
Wood Dragons are generally creative, engaging and beautiful to behold, full of elegance, style and refined taste. As such they are naturals in the highest social circles. They usually marry well and spend their time directing public charity events.
Years of birth: 1964, 2024

THE WOOD SNAKE ~ Wood fuels Fire: Sensuality & sexuality
Wood Snakes may give in to laziness and indulgence in sensual delights rather than accomplishing anything outside of their own needs. Career, power and influence are not as important to Wood Snakes as they are to other Snakes, so they can fall far short of their true potential. **Years of birth: 1965, 2025**

THE WOOD HORSE ~ Fire is controlled by Water: Recklessness tamed
Wood Horses are more relaxed and less excitable than other Horses. They demonstrate stability in all facets of life, from romance to career. Wood Horses are cooperative and caring, and tend to be gullible. **Year of birth: 1954, 2014**

THE WOOD SHEEP ~ Earth controls Wood: Stability & direction
Wood Sheep are extremely creative and artistic. Unmotivated by money or fame, they spend all their time on creative and artistic pursuits. Generous to a fault, Wood Sheep are compassionate and caring. **Years of birth: 1955, 2015**

THE WOOD MONKEY ~ Wood is controlled by Metal: Strength & domination
Wood Monkeys are more balanced and less volatile than other Monkeys, with a methodical approach to solving problems. These Monkeys are more capable of specific achievements and less attracted to practical jokes. **Years of birth: 1944, 2004**

THE WOOD ROOSTER ~ Wood is controlled by Metal: Expansion
Wood Roosters show an early interest in personal growth and take every opportunity to challenge their own beliefs and explore other options.
They are keen seekers of knowledge and their homes are full of half-read books. Wood Roosters are more flexible and adaptable than other Roosters.
Years of birth: 1945, 2005

THE WOOD DOG ~ Earth is utilised by Wood: Personal growth
Wood Dogs are more fun loving and optimistic than other Dogs. They are open to life's experiences, willing to change their values and principles. Wood Dogs, deeply empathetic, place fewer expectations on themselves. **Years of birth: 1934, 1994**

THE WOOD PIG ~ From Water grows Wood: Enhancing combination
Wood gives Pigs the opportunity for total self-expression. Wood Pigs can talk, and talk, and talk. They need to consider careers where their verbal talents can be appreciated. Sometimes Wood Pigs can be too quick to express their opinions and need to consciously avoid offense. **Years of birth: 1935, 1955.**

Born in a Fire Year

1916, 1917, 1926, 1927, 1936, 1937, 1966, 1967, 1976, 1977, 1966, 1967, 1976, 1977, 1986, 1987, 1996, 1997, 2006, 2007, 2016, 2017

Passion, energy, decisiveness, and enthusiasm.

THE FIRE RAT ~ Fire is controlled by Water: Opportunity to control the darker side
Fire Rats are always on the go both physically and mentally, finding it hard to slow down or even take a rest. Fire Rats are more forthright and passionately outspoken than other Rats and do not usually suffer from this sign's inclination toward stress and anxiety. **Years of birth: 1936, 1996**

THE FIRE OX ~ From Fire comes Earth: Powerfully enhancing
This is one Ox you want as a friend and never as an enemy. Fire Oxen have volatile personalities and can pack quite a force both physically and verbally when challenged or confronted. For all their huff and puff, they are also full of enthusiasm and passion. **Years of birth: 1937, 1997**

THE FIRE TIGER ~ From Wood comes Fire: Passion & energy
Fire Tigers exhibit enormous energy and magnetism. They are courageous, taking unthinkable risks. Fire Tigers pack a lot of activity and adventure into their lives and want constant change in their careers and relationships. **Years of birth: 1926, 1986**

THE FIRE HARE ~ From Wood comes Fire: Passion & energy
Gusto, courage and motivation are just what Hares require to really get going. Fire Hares are the most successful Hares in high-profile professions. They are able to blend intuition and reflection with personal magnetism, and are often hugely popular individuals. **Years of birth: 1927, 1987**

THE FIRE DRAGON ~ From Fire comes Earth: Powerfully enhancing
Fire Dragons appear like bolts of lightning — magnetic, magnificent, energizing, and awe-inspiring. They are totally aware of their effect on others and take pleasure in it. Their life is full of dazzling social engagements, interesting people, and exciting places. **Years of birth: 1916, 1976**

THE FIRE SNAKE ~ Double Fire: Energy & dynamism

Double Fire gives these Snakes all the physical resources they require to match their superior intellects. Fire Snakes are unstoppable in business and will achieve high status quickly and with ease. **Years of birth: 1917, 1977**

THE FIRE HORSE ~ Double Fire: Energy & dynamism

Double Fire blows the energy meters off these Horses. They are hurried, daring and restless. Fire Horses have numerous projects on the go at one time and find it hard to concentrate on detail or a methodical approach. They will also find commitment difficult and are more comfortable single. **Year of birth: 1966, 2026**

THE FIRE SHEEP ~ From Fire comes Earth: Powerfully enhancing

Fire Sheep have the willpower and motivation to achieve their goals. Unlike other Sheep who are more idle and placid, Fire Sheep are confident and have a warm, caring and winning personality. Fire Sheep make appealing socialites and good networkers. **Year of birth: 1967**

THE FIRE MONKEY ~ Metal is moulded by Fire: Intensity & direction

Fire Monkeys are focused on power and control from an early age. This is not a personality given to compassion and sense of fair play. They can be ruthless, and have flexible values and principles if necessary. **Years of birth: 1956, 2016**

THE FIRE ROOSTER ~ Metal is moulded by Fire: Intensity & direction

Fire Roosters are bold, direct and blunt. They can appear extremely loud and colorful. Fire Roosters like to make dramatic entrances, parade across grand dance floors and generally be the focus of attention. **Years of birth: 1957, 2017**

THE FIRE DOG ~ From Fire comes Earth: Powerful and enhancing

Fire Dogs do not lose sight of their own needs and desires like other Dog types. They are passionate about humanitarian causes and quietly confident in their ability to make a real difference. They require little effort to win others' support, and generally lead a comfortable, emotionally fulfilled life. **Years of birth: 1946, 2006**

THE FIRE PIG ~ Fire is controlled by Water: Action

Fire Pigs are proactive, confident and motivated enough to aim for specific goals. They can be too keen to win others' approval, which can lead to danger. They need to practice more patience to ensure their own safety. **Years of birth: 1947, 2007**

Born in an Earth Year

1918, 1919, 1928, 1929, 1938, 1939, 1988, 1989, 1998, 1999, 1968, 1969, 1978, 1979, 1988, 1989, 1998, 1999, 2008, 2009, 2018, 2019

Balance, wisdom, patience, and practicality.

THE EARTH RAT ~ Water is controlled by Earth: Stability & direction
Earth Rats are logical realists who reflect carefully before making any decisions. Full of good advice, Earth Rats rarely make a wrong move and give valuable advice to family, friends and business associates. They appear satisfied and at peace with life's ups and downs. **Years of birth: 1948, 2008**

THE EARTH OX ~ Double Earth: Practicality & worldly wisdom
Earth Oxen are wise, practical and patient. They can be quite resourceful when it comes to solving problems, and often achieve their aims. Being able to engage with their emotions is their main challenge. **Years of birth: 1949, 2009**

THE EARTH TIGER ~ Earth is utilized by Wood: Core strengths harnessed
Earth Tigers have more common sense, patience and practicality than other Tigers. They are stable individuals who value the security of a solid foundation — a job, a home to call their own and caring friends and family. **Years of birth: 1938, 1998**

THE EARTH HARE ~ Earth is utilized by Wood: Core strengths harnessed
Traditionalist Earth Hares tend to be inflexible about ethics, values and principles. They can be prudish and judgmental. They work hard for their cherished security and do not take risks. **Years of birth: 1939, 1999**

THE EARTH DRAGON ~ Double Earth: Practicality & worldly wisdom
Earth Dragons are more sedate and calm than other Dragons. Their lives are less chaotic as they are able to recognize and follow wise counsel. They are practical, realistic and emotionally balanced. **Years of birth: 1928, 1988**

THE EARTH SNAKE — From Fire comes Earth: Powerful & enhancing
Earth Snakes are gentle souls with no hidden agendas. They radiate tranquility and calm. Their genuine care for others is demonstrated in their open communication style. They make good facilitators and counselors. **Years of birth: 1929, 1989**

THE EARTH HORSE ~ From Fire comes Earth: Powerful & enhancing
Earth Horses are able to find the stability and focus often missing in Horses' lives. They are resourceful, and will apply their energy to achieving long-term goals. Earth Horses are blessed with a balance of worldly wisdom and youthful exuberance. **Years of birth: 1918, 1978**

THE EARTH SHEEP ~ Double Earth: Practicality & worldly wisdom
Earth Sheep are focused on achieving spiritual fulfilment throughout their lives. They have a strong spiritual side. Earth Sheep are truly caring and compassionate souls, willing to sacrifice much in order to better the lives of others. **Years of birth: 1919, 1979**

THE EARTH MONKEY ~ From Earth comes Metal: Engaging & activating
Earth Monkeys are more interested in lending their mental dexterity to useful pursuits than to fun and games. They are interested in lifelong learning, taking evening classes and acquiring many qualifications. **Years of birth: 1968, 2028**

THE EARTH ROOSTER ~ From Earth comes Metal: Engaging and activating
Earth provides the usually flamboyant Rooster with much needed reserve in both dress and communication style. Earth Roosters do not avoid accountability. They are practical and grounded, full of common sense and responsibility. **Years of birth: 1969, 2029**

THE EARTH DOG ~ Double Earth: Emphasis on balance and worldly wisdom
Earth emphasizes these Dogs' reliability and steadfast devotion, and ensures they do not fall prey to depression and self-doubt. Earth Dogs are therefore more able to take negative blows. They take their commitments seriously. **Years of birth: 1958, 2018**

THE EARTH PIG ~ Water is controlled by Earth: Groundedness & direction
Earth Pigs make natural homemakers. They desire security, and do not value careers, travel or an adventurous life. Earth Pigs are happiest when married with children and comfortably settled in their family home. They take much pleasure in the daily routines of family life. **Year of birth: 1959, 2019**

Interpreting Chinese Astrology

Chinese astrology provides useful insights into our individual characters, strengths and weaknesses, and helps us to understand how we relate to others. You need only a date and time of birth, and you will be able to determine and analyze the following crucial elements of a Chinese astrology profile:

- the traits provided by the animals ruling the date and time of birth
- the energies present (yin or yang),
- the set of natural and dominant elements

Year of Birth = Dominant Sign

If you want to get a general idea of your personality, or that of others, all you need to start with is the year of birth, and the element associated with it (see the List of Years and Astrology Signs on pages 78–79). These factors will provide a detailed description of your external character — the one that you project to others.

Time of Birth = Ascendant Sign

The animal sign ruling over the time of your birth is your **ascendant sign**. Like the element that governs your year, it modifies the characteristics of your dominant sign. The ascendant sign indicates your hidden self. This is the way you perceive yourself, and is the side you will conceal from others. Note: a **pure sign** occurs when the dominant and ascendant signs are the same.

Month of Birth = Love Sign

The traits of this animal sign reveal your character in intimate relationships. Knowing these traits will help you uncover a more detailed profile which will help you to find a truly compatible partner.

Example ~ Steve

Date of Birth: 29/11/63

Time: 8.30am

Dominant sign & element: Water Hare
Element: wood. Energy: yin.

Ascendant sign: Dragon
(Note: the ascendant sign is based on your time of birth).
Element: Earth. Energy: yang.

Love sign: Pig
(Note: The love sign is based on your month of birth).
Element: Water. Energy: Yin.

Energies: Yin ~ Yang ~ Yin
Steve's profile shows a good balance between yin and yang energies.
His personality is neither introverted nor extroverted, but he has a
preference for introversion.

Animal signs: Hare ~ Dragon ~ Pig
The mix of animal signs ensures Steve has a comprehensive array of
character traits, with a leaning toward the "cooperatives" affinity group
(see page 75). The Dragon ascendant assures him strength and willpower
when necessary.

Elements: Wood ~ Earth ~ Water
Steve's mix of elements is positive, harmonious and centered on the
softer, more creative elements, wood and water. As there is no fire or
metal present, Steve is quite easy-going and artistic but with a practical,
realistic mindset (influence of the earth element).

Relating to Rats

Life Roles

FRIEND

Rats' considerate and supportive nature makes them good friends. They like helping close friends where they can, with advice, personal coaching or money. As Rats value loyalty, they tend to have only a few close friends, although they do like being entertained by numerous acquaintances. Rats are particularly fond of praise and open demonstrations of appreciation, which is all a friend to a Rat needs to provide in return.

RELATIVE

Rats are excellent at providing for their families financially, and take their responsibilities as caretakers seriously. They want to be leaders within their families, encouraging and supporting partners and children. They take a democratic approach to decision making but need to feel they have significant influence, if not control, within the home, particularly given their thrift, wisdom and sensitivity.

LOVER

(Those born in a Rat year and/or during the month of December.) Rats are innovative when it comes to wooing their chosen mates. If you like a partner who attends to the little details of romance and seduction and who takes great pride in personal appearance, then a Rat is for you. As Rats are usually afflicted by personal insecurities, they will be attracted to committed, long-term relationships that provide them with plenty of emotional support.

WORKER

Best career choices: chief executive, chartered accountant, stockbroker, lawyer, politician. Rats are at home in the world of business. With a keen intellect and obvious competence, they seek out occupations that engage them fully and make good use of their mental dexterity. It is not uncommon to see intuitive Rats swiftly elevated to the top. They need visible recognition for their hard work to maintain their loyalty.

PERSONAL NEEDS

Rats need copious amounts of attention, recognition and praise; otherwise they will quickly focus their energies elsewhere to address their personal insecurities.

Relationships

Positive pairing

RAT & MONKEY mentally engaging
Each admires the other's mental dexterity and artful communication style. They can accomplish much together, and address each other's need for support and understanding.

RAT & DRAGON dynamic & charismatic
A high-energy and magnetic combination that will keep both partners on their toes. They have common desires, values and outlook on life. With such rapport, both will attain success.

RAT & RAT security focused
A meeting of like minds and an easy camaraderie for both friends or colleagues. But both are too focused on security and introspection, making it difficult to support each other emotionally.

RAT & OX mutually rewarding
An ideal balance between Rat's intelligence and Ox's perseverance and tenacity. Together they can achieve much success, and acquire wealth. Both need to take time out and enjoy romance.

RAT & HARE good taste & calm abound
Useful pairing. Both are intelligent, articulate and stylish, which ensures a comfortable relationship regardless of context.

RAT & SNAKE ambitious & innovative
A relationship focused on material wealth and financial gain. Both will encourage the other's development and success in life.

RAT & PIG initially resourceful
While Rats will earn their keep, Pigs are just as quick to spend it. The Rat initially feels appreciated in this breadwinner role, but can soon tire of Pig's indulgences.

RAT & DOG mutually respectful
Harmony probable. Rats appreciate Dogs' loyalty and respect their morality. Dogs feel inspired by Rats' ambition. As both are prone to insecurities and self-doubt, the relationship can hit low points.

Negative pairing

RAT & TIGER clash of values & ideals
Where the patient Rat wants time to reflect, the Tiger will be impatient for action. This will mean mutual frustration. Unless they can appreciate the benefits of each other's approach, this relationship will not be a long-term success.

RAT & HORSE agitated & frustrating
Both are egotistical and want control. The Rat wants to tame the freedom loving Horse, which the Horse will resent. The Rat will feel insecure with the Horse's constant wandering and change in direction.

RAT & SHEEP lacks long-term interest
Initial attraction possible, but Sheep are too indulgent for work-oriented Rats. Sheep value freedom, creativity and love, and Rats value hard work, possessions and financial security.

RAT & ROOSTER heated debates ensue
No attraction likely. Rats do not care for Roosters' flamboyance and bluntness. Roosters become bored with Rats' pristine presentation and conformist nature.

On Good Terms with an Ox

Life Roles

FRIEND

As friends Oxen are considerate and jovial. They like to spend their rare leisure moments with a small group of trusted friends who like indulging in food and wine and appreciating the arts. They are skilled chefs and love giving dinner parties. They are accomplished hosts, able to attend to all their guests' requirements without stress. Oxen are valued for their easy company and practical advice.

RELATIVE

Oxen make very grounded, practical and dependable family members. They truly appreciate their homes and families. Traditionalists at heart, they want the very best for and from their family members, which can make them quite demanding. They work day and night to ensure the family's financial security, but may not be as attentive to their emotional needs.

LOVER

(Those born in an Ox year and/or during the month of January.) The Ox is not a passionate or romantic sign. As they focus more on work than love, Oxen are not likely to experience numerous sexually charged relationships. They do have an eye for beauty, can be quite sensuous, and have lots of stamina in bed. Not overly demonstrative in public, they will show how much they care by staying monogamous and providing a secure home for the loved one.

WORKER

Best career choices: judge, police officer, administrator, ambulance driver, government worker. Work is the area of life Oxen feel totally prepared for and comfortable in. Trustworthy and respected for their methodical and detailed approach to projects, they are often viewed as generous and dependable, particularly by colleagues and superiors. Oxen will have little trouble securing promotions and pay raises, and this is due to sheer merit. They tend to set high expectations for themselves and others.

PERSONAL NEEDS

Oxen need to be appreciated for their hard work and dependability.

Relationships

Positive pairing

OX & ROOSTER harmonious & balanced

A successful pairing. The socially oriented Rooster does not have to compete for the limelight, and the Ox is relieved of this responsibility and can concentrate on the more serious areas of life.

OX & SNAKE long-term success

Both have patience and a structured approach to work and responsibilities; they will feel a natural balance and harmony. When they reach for their goals, the Ox will provide the physical resources, the Snake the intuition and reflection.

OX & RAT mutually rewarding

An ideal balance between the Rat's intelligence and the Ox's perseverance and tenacity. They complement each other well, and together can gain much success and acquire wealth. Both need to take time out and enjoy romance.

OX & HARE potentially useful

The Ox has ample room to control and dominate in this relationship, and will be grateful for the Hare's calm, relaxed manner. The Hare truly appreciates the Ox's attention to security issues.

OX & DOG mutually respectful

Both are traditionalists and highly principled, and respect and admire each other immensely. They will need to take a lighter approach at times to ensure life does not become too serious.

OX & OX all work & little play likely

While this can work in the long run, two Oxen together means too much hard work and too little fun. Both will need to make considerable effort to communicating their emotional needs.

OX & MONKEY lacks sufficient trust

Oxen are usually quick to admire Monkeys' devilish manner, which Monkeys will reward with a little attention. Attraction between them is usually only superficial.

OX & PIG only peaceful initially

Both require harmonious surroundings to be productive. Both provide peace and quiet, but the Pig's indulgence and lack of restraint can cause friction.

Negative pairing

TIGER & OX natural enemies in the wild

Both the Ox and the Tiger like control and will want to dominate. The Chinese say it takes two Tigers to kill an Ox, which says a lot about this volatile and quite physically oriented pairing.

OX & DRAGON clashes abound

Both will feel they have met their match early in this union. However, the Ox will eventually feel ignored by the self-centered Dragon, who will quickly be bored with the Ox's conservatism.

OX & HORSE ineffective communication

Both signs have conflicting speeds and approaches to life. The Horse is lively and sees life as a fun adventure, while the Ox is more deliberate and takes a more serious view.

OX & SHEEP opposing values

Sheep are too emotional and sensitive for logical and forthright Oxen. Sheep are too easily influenced into indulgences, which principled Oxen frown upon. No respect likely.

Trying Life with a Tiger

Life Roles

FRIEND
Optimistic, jovial and charismatic. Blessed with a sunny disposition, and dislike for wallowing in the negative, they are extremely supportive and uplifting to friends who suffer from ill health or bad times. Their impressive array of traits make most Tigers extremely popular at social gatherings, where they will often be the life of the party.

RELATIVE
Extremely protective and generous with their loved ones. Often seen as childish by others, due to their engaging presence and energetic approach to life. They are wonderfully natural, inspiring and encouraging with children, and are often the favorite aunt/uncle. Make great parents themselves, provided they can balance their time with the children with time away from the family home.

LOVER
(Those born in a Tiger year and/or during the month of February.) The courageous and passionate lovers of the Chinese zodiac. Full of zest and personal charisma. Romp from one romance to another, never quite satisfied, on the lookout for someone unusual or different. Ruled by their hearts, they follow their instincts when it comes to romance. Rarely employ logic or reflect on the new object of their affection. Attraction to adventure and the unusual will keep many Tigers single until well into middle age.

WORKER
Best career choices: actor, business owner, writer, union leader, explorer, teacher, military leader. Tigers' key strengths in the workplace are their infectious motivation and enthusiasm. With a keen sense of urgency, they like to get things done quickly. They make formidable business leaders who can quickly rise to high positions, provided that they follow the wise counsel of those they trust. Their loyalty and compassion for their colleagues will ensure their popularity spills over from their social to their professional lives.

PERSONAL NEEDS
Tigers need to relax and be pampered, and they need to be persuaded to take time out occasionally from their hectic lifestyles.

Relationships

Positive pairing

TIGER & HORSE passionate & exhilarating
Horses and Tigers share the same values and outlook on life. The Horse finds it easy to motivate the Tiger to greater accomplishment, while the Tiger knows how to reward the Horse.

TIGER & DOG mutual respect
Complete harmony between impetuous Tiger and patient Dog. Mutual respect of the other's values, as well as respect for each other's courage.

TIGER & HARE differences attract
The reticent Hare is happy for the Tiger to take control. The Hare will appreciate the Tiger's differences and the Tiger will feel supported by the Hare.

TIGER & DRAGON charismatic
Both have magnetism to burn and the relationship will motivate both of these extreme extroverts. However, sharing the limelight is not enough for these daring individuals and the relationship could breed jealousy.

TIGER & PIG life's a party
The Pig will rule the home and appreciate the Tiger's need to roam the world outside. These two fall naturally into their most cherished roles — homemaker Pig and provider Tiger.

TIGER & TIGER danger & impulsiveness
A magnetic attraction exists between two exuberant Tigers. However, the union will be fraught with recklessness due to their lack of patience and realism.

TIGER & SHEEP sexually fuelled
Only have their sex drive in common. In the bedroom, they will please each other immensely. Elsewhere, no rapport or respect.

TIGER & ROOSTER initially captivating
Drawn together instantly, as they appear bold and entertaining to each other. Rooster will demand perfection, which reckless Tiger cannot deliver. Tiger will find Rooster suffocating.

Negative pairing

TIGER & SNAKE misunderstandings ensue
The curious Tiger is easily draw in by the Snake's mesmerizing appearance. However, the Snake will not value the Tiger's boundless energy and lack of forethought. The Tiger will find the Snake cold and deceitful.

TIGER & MONKEY traps abound
Monkey has the most delightful prey in the impetuous Tiger, and will draw the Tiger into danger too often. The Tiger encourages the worst in the Monkey's behavior.

TIGER & RAT clash of values & ideals
The patient Rat will take time out to reflect; the Tiger will be impatient for action. This means mutual frustration. No long-term success unless they can appreciate the benefits of each other's approach to life.

TIGER & OX natural enemies in the wild
Both the Ox and the Tiger like control and will want to dominate. The Chinese say it takes two Tigers to kill an Ox, which says a lot about this volatile and quite physically oriented pairing.

Harmonizing with Hares

Life Roles

FRIEND

Flexible, easy to get along with. Detest confrontation, prefer to reason out any disagreements. Do not place great demands on their friends. As Hares are more introverted than extroverted, they prefer the company of small, intimate groups to large exciting parties. Like to entertain in style and at a leisurely pace.

RELATIVE

Demonstrate a taste for the finer things in life when it comes to their homes. Have good taste and a keen eye for valuable objects. Their homes are showpieces. Comfort is a high priority to these sensuous creatures. Responsible and calm parents who value harmony in family relations. Do not operate well in volatile situations. Will quickly leave any relationship that threatens their own or their children's security and well-being.

LOVER

(Those born in a Hare year and/or during the month of March.) Hares are renowned for their sensual orientation in China. Extremely sexy, irresistible in affairs of the heart. Sensitive, indulgent and romantic, and will invest much time and energy in their intimate relationships. Will expect the same from their partners. Hares' discretion and introversion are well-suited to illicit affairs, although they are normally attracted to confident, successful partners who meet their need for social status.

WORKER

Best career choices: antique dealer, interior decorator, art collector, diplomat, sociologist. Require autonomy and quiet surroundings in order to perform at their best. Independent roles suit them well, where they can operate at their own comfortable and even pace. Any occupation in the arts will suit them, particularly roles that call on their refined good taste. Make successful mediators due to their intuition and intelligence.

PERSONAL NEEDS

Hares need to take account of their delicate senses, and seek a quiet, peaceful environment in which to rest and reflect.

Relationships

Positive pairing

HARE & PIG a winning pair
Both are considerate and peace loving. Together they can create the gentle harmony each requires. From this comfortable base both can succeed in their individual projects.

HARE & SHEEP a nurturing union
Openly show love for each other, and keen to nurture the other's well-being. The Hare gets the Sheep organized, the Sheep provides the Hare with sensual delights.

HARE & RAT good taste & calm abound
Both Rats and Hares are intelligent, articulate and stylish, which ensures a comfortable relationship regardless of context.

HARE & OX potentially useful
Oxen have ample room to control and dominate in this relationship, and will be grateful for Hares' calm and relaxed manner. Hares will appreciate Oxen's attention to security issues.

HARE & TIGER differences attract
Reticent Hares are happy for Tigers to take control. Hares will appreciate Tigers' differences and Tigers will feel supported by Hares.

HARE & HARE polite & cooperative
Polite, civil relationship. Both are relaxed, and naturally understand and attend to the other's needs. However, the relationship cannot deal well with outside pressure.

HARE & SNAKE good taste abounds
Mutual traits are emphasized; both will be happy. Both desire and will strive together for the finer things in life and the company of the social elite.

HARE & DOG mutual sharing
Tempers will rarely flare. Each will be happy to make sacrifices for the other. While harmonious and considerate, the union can lack initiative.

Negative pairing

HARE & MONKEY civil to a point
Will appreciate each other's intelligence and social wit, but have opposing values. The Hare seeks to blend with others, the Monkey to stand apart.

HARE & DRAGON too extreme
The dynamic Dragon is too overpowering and volatile for the balanced and harmonious Hare. There is little for each other in this union except frustration and stress on Hare's part.

HARE & HORSE differences irritate
Frustration and lack of communication. The energetic and fiery Horse will lose patience with the steady pace and passivity of the Hare.

HARE & ROOSTER total misunderstanding
Roosters are frank, regardless of the consequences. Hares will keep their opinions to themselves for peace. Hares will find Roosters intolerable, Roosters find Hares insincere.

Dealing with Dragons

Life Roles

FRIEND

Outgoing, engaging and extroverted. Need lots of friends and social activities to stimulate their excitable natures. Their friends will also need to be upbeat and adventurous, or Dragons will soon tire and move on to more attractive acquaintances. Dragons do not need deep and long-term friendships — they have ample self-confidence and a bevy of admirers.

RELATIVE

Dragons find it hard to separate family and social life. So, their homes are full of people coming and going. Dragon children have scholarly and sporting talents and can make significant progress if sufficiently motivated. As parents, they keep their families very busy in a variety of activities and travels, as they detest the idea of a routine existence. Not attracted to fussy furnishings and will need to live in wide open spaces.

LOVER

(Those born in a Dragon year and/or during the month of April.) Magnificent lovers due to their high energy and vibrant personalities. Need to be loved and relish the adoration of others, particularly those they are attracted to. Hence, they will fall in love frequently if for no other reason but to continue the euphoria a new relationship brings. This compulsion for the new and exciting leaves Dragons with only a short-term focus. However, as they mature the idea of commitment will be more appealing.

WORKER

Best career choices: visual artist, photographic journalist, adventurer, athlete, artist, company director, entrepreneur, military position. Being at the very top is what Dragons do best. Chief executive officer, managing director and senior partner are all titles befitting their ideal leadership traits. Dragons have vision and can operate well strategically in business. They take control, and refuse to play second fiddle to others.

PERSONAL NEEDS

As Dragons can sometimes question their own magnificence and obvious talents, they do need to hear sincere appraisals of their competence on occasion.

Relationships

Positive pairing

DRAGON & RAT dynamic & charismatic
A high-energy, magnetic combination which keeps both partners on their toes. They have common desires, values and outlook on life. With such rapport both will attain success.

DRAGON & MONKEY inventive & lively
Drawn to each other — Dragons to Monkeys for their social flair and innovation, and Monkeys to Dragons for their charisma and confidence. Dragons will rule, Monkeys will toe the line. A successful relationship.

DRAGON & TIGER charismatic
Both have magnetism to burn and the relationship will motivate both of these extreme extroverts. However, sharing the limelight is not enough for these daring individuals and the relationship could breed jealousy.

DRAGON & SNAKE socially beneficial
Dragon will appreciate Snake's beauty and networking talents in social situations. Snake will feel uplifted and energized by Dragon's presence and personal appeal.

DRAGON & HORSE active & vital
Each encourages the other into accomplishing more. Provided they can be practical in their daily activities and take time to rest, this relationship could be harmonious.

DRAGON & PIG surprisingly successful
Little in common. However, in a gregarious mood, Dragon will sweep awestruck Pig into the air, and both will be happy with Dragon in command.

DRAGON & DRAGON magnetic
Two Dragons together is just too much. Dragons need to be center stage and in control. Neither will relent, and power struggles will ensue. Each will see in the other the best and worst of themselves.

DRAGON & ROOSTER superficial
Both are colorful, hence initial attraction is guaranteed. However, both are too self-obsessed to give what is required for building and sustaining a committed relationship.

Negative pairing

DRAGON & HARE too extreme
The dynamic Dragon is too overpowering and volatile for the balanced and harmonious Hare. There is little for each other in this union except frustration and stress on Hare's part.

DRAGON & OX clashes abound
Both will feel they have met their match early in this union. However, the Ox will eventually feel ignored by the self-centered Dragon, who will quickly be bored with the Ox's conservatism.

DRAGON & SHEEP opposing desires
Little will mutually attract or inspire. Dragon is focused on the big picture and goal accomplishment, Sheep lives for the moment.

DRAGON & DOG differences do not impress
Dogs are too serious and judgmental for the optimistic, entertaining Dragon, who likes breaking the rules. The Dragon will misbehave endlessly to frustrate the Dog even further.

Succeeding with Snakes

Life Roles

FRIEND
Snakes are the skilled networkers of the Chinese zodiac. They make use of every social gathering to develop contacts and are adept at camouflaging their intent. They do build honest friendships with others — it's just that they seem to get more use out of their alliances than just friendship. They prefer artistic and cultural gatherings to sports or overly active, competitive gatherings. Good entertainers and delight in holding formal dinner parties.

RELATIVE
Snakes cherish their homes for the stability and protection they provide. Snakes know that family ties are useful for support. Hence, they spend a lot of time and energy on creating just the right environment. They pay attention to detail and have good taste in furnishing; they will manage the family's budget well. Once settled, they make caring parents who are sensitive to their children's and partners' needs.

LOVER
(Those born in a Snake year and/or during the month of May.) In the East, Snakes are renowned for their hypnotic beauty and seductive streak, and are able to mesmerize everyone around them. They like to settle down quickly with someone they perceive can meet their high personal and social criteria. Given their clear agenda in matters of the heart, they can come across as cool and distant. However, once committed they are capable of deep emotions.

WORKER
Best career choices: professor, critic, writer, human resource manager, interior designer, scientist. Snakes are assured of professional success, given their ability to detach emotionally from situations, and their adaptability. They will seek out positions where they can influence the apparent power brokers, and quietly relish their manipulative skills in all-important strategic matters. Their business acumen and intuition will ensure they never fall prey to corporate traps.

PERSONAL NEEDS
Snakes need to know they can influence others and hold their respect for the advice they give. Tell them how smart they are, and how beneficial their counsel has been.

Relationships

Positive pairing

SNAKE & OX long-term success
Both have patience and a structured approach to their work and responsibilities. In reaching for their goals, Oxen will provide the physical resources, Snakes the intuition and reflection.

SNAKE & ROOSTER perfect complements
Snake admires Rooster's extravagance, colorful appearance and intelligent conversation. Rooster is smart enough to appreciate Snake's wisdom and follow the counsel offered.

SNAKE & RAT ambitious & innovative
A relationship focused on material wealth and financial gain. Both will encourage the other's development and success in life.

SNAKE & HARE good taste abounds
Mutual traits are emphasized; both will be happy. Both desire and will strive together for the finer things in life and the company of the social elite.

SNAKE & DRAGON socially beneficial
Dragons will appreciate Snakes' beauty and networking talents in social situations. Snakes will feel uplifted and energized by Dragons' presence and personal appeal.

SNAKE & MONKEY ingenuity abounds
This pairing of the most intelligent signs is sure to breed ingenuity and innovation. Particularly useful as a business relationship. Snakes and Monkeys are able to predict future trends and take well-calculated risks.

SNAKE & SHEEP platonically cultured
Snake and Sheep suit each other well as friends due to their similar interests. However, Sheep are too sensitive for the usually detached Snake and will not feel comfortable in an intimate relationship.

SNAKE & SNAKE hypnotic dilemma
Snakes can be too reflective at times, and miss opportunities for action. Two Snakes together can breed laziness. While they can hatch brilliant plans and detailed actions together, neither can motivate or encourage the other.

Negative pairing

SNAKE & TIGER misunderstandings ensue
The curious Tiger is easily draw in by the Snake's mesmerizing appearance. However, the Snake will not value the Tiger's boundless energy and lack of forethought. The Tiger will find the Snake cold and deceitful.

SNAKE & HORSE superficial attraction
Beautiful Snakes and physically fit, youthful Horses attract each other. However, Snakes are prone to jealousy, and freedom-loving Horses will feel stifled.

SNAKE & DOG misunderstood intentions
Snakes will lead and Dogs follow obediently. But secretive Snakes will be too much for upfront Dogs to understand. Snakes will eventually tire of Dogs' moralizing.

SNAKE & PIG lacking appreciation
Pigs are easy to read, as they hold nothing back and live for the moment. Snakes are hard to read and cautious. A relationship between the two is virtually impossible.

Happiness with the Horse

Life Roles

FRIEND

Horses keep their friends on the move. Horses have no need for relaxing holidays and leisurely lunches; they demand real activity. They are talkative, and often gossips, and will provide entertaining tales over the dinner table. Aside from physical activity, they are more giving than demanding in their friendships.

RELATIVE

Horses are the energetic youngsters who refuse to grow up. They bring energy, activity, fun and encouragement to a family in any role, whether it be parent, sibling, partner or child. Horses leave the family nest early to feed their worldly curiosity and adventurous spirit. It is rare for Horses to settle down early in life. But when they do, they are quite protective of their families and cherish their children's company.

LOVER

(Those born in a Horse year and/or in the month of June.) Horses are virile and physically exhausting as lovers. Blessed with youthful vitality and enthusiasm, Horses leap into love affairs with wild abandon. This doesn't seem to bother them or their partners: what they lack in foresight they make up for in vitality and magnetism. Unfortunately their attention span does not encourage long-term commitments. Horses are forever restless for change and variety, and have promiscuous lifestyles.

WORKER

Best career choices: photojournalist, traveling salesperson, builder, rally driver, tour operator. Horses are dexterous and can work at a furious pace. This suits them to the trades, where they are appreciated for their productivity. Horses are also talkative, and genuinely like to be around new and interesting people. They make great salespeople and customer service providers. Their restlessness, need for variety and attraction to the outdoors will see them changing jobs frequently.

PERSONAL NEEDS

Horses need adoration and lots of space in their relationships, and constant stimulation in their work.

Relationships

Positive pairing

HORSE & TIGER passionate & exhilarating

Horses and Tigers share the same values and outlook on life. The Horse finds it easy to motivate the Tiger to greater accomplishment, while the Tiger knows how to reward the Horse.

HORSE & DOG supportive & loving

Admire each other's physical engagement with life. Likely to form a successful long-term relationship due to their protective and openly affectionate natures.

HORSE & HORSE happily non-committed

It's hard to tell when these two are in a relationship, as both lead such independent lives. Provided they take some time out to do things together and don't ask for too much from each other, the relationship will work well.

HORSE & SHEEP mutual interests

Horses are creative and Sheep are artistic. Together they can create beautiful things. Sheep need to be content with less emotional support from Horses to keep the union happy.

HORSE & MONKEY energetic flexibility

Monkeys likes Horses' enthusiasm and talkative nature, and Horses likes Monkeys' wit and fun approach. However, Horses can be naive and gullible, and Monkeys will find taking advantage irresistible.

HORSE & PIG socially active & popular

Both like having a good time and will maintain a hectic social life. Provided Pigs do not overly indulge, Horses will stay interested.

HORSE & DRAGON active & vital

Each encourages and coaxes the other into accomplishing more. Provided they can be practical in their daily activities and take time to rest, this relationship could be harmonious.

HORSE & ROOSTER socially active

An entertaining pair, exuberant and attracted to the social set. At some stage Rooster's need for structure will try to dominate, and then Horse will run.

Negative pairing

HORSE & SNAKE superficial attraction

Beautiful Snakes and physically fit, youthful Horses attract each other. However, Snakes are prone to jealousy and freedom-loving Horses will feel stifled.

HORSE & OX ineffective communication

Conflicting approaches to life. Horses are lively and see life as a fun adventure. Oxen are more deliberate, taking a more serious view.

HORSE & HARE differences irritate

Frustration and lack of communication. Energetic, fiery Horses will lose patience with the steady pace and passivity of Hares.

HORSE & RAT agitated & frustrating

Both are egotistical and want control. Rats want to tame freedom-loving Horses, which Horses resent. Horses' constant wandering makes Rats feel insecure.

Sharing Life with a Sheep

Life Roles

FRIEND

As peacemakers and generous spirits, Sheep are valued by their friends and their company is sought in difficult times. Sheep take a parental approach in their friendships, and feel acutely the need to support friends both emotionally and financially. They are loyal and totally accepting of differences, and expect their friends to be there when their own situations call for a shoulder to cry on.

RELATIVE

Sheep love being part of a group, and a close-knit family is ideal. Once married, Sheep cherish the continued security and closeness, and go to great lengths to ensure the family's emotional stability. Sheep homes are full of warmth and love; soft furnishings and gold-framed family portraits abound. Naturals in the parental role, they are patient and skilled at nurturing and communicating with young minds.

LOVER

(Those born in a Sheep year and/or during the month of July.) Sheep are sensuous, with very active sex drives. They are in tune with their own feelings and desires and intuitive with their partners' needs. Compassionate and understanding, Sheep are romantic and expect generosity and attention. They can express their own needs and desires and ensure they are met. In love with love, Sheep will explore a variety of lovers before committing.

WORKER

Best career choices: writer, poet, musician, artist, actor, therapist, religious minister, gardener. Sheep are popular at work with employers and colleagues alike and take a flexible, friendly, easy-going approach to work and work relationships. Not excessively career-oriented, Sheep are happy to remain involved in people issues or creative pursuits rather than politics. They are good with detail and at analyzing problem areas.

PERSONAL NEEDS

Sheep need a supportive, stress-free environment at home and at work.

Relationships

Positive pairing

SHEEP & HARE a nurturing union
Openly show love for each other, keen to nurture the other's well-being. Hares get Sheep organized, Sheep provide Hares with sensual delights.

SHEEP & PIG supportive & creative
Both can provide the comfort and nurturing atmosphere the other needs most. A carefree existence, encouraging and supportive of each other's talents.

SHEEP & DOG tolerant & beneficial
Both are compassionate, patient and sensitive, and willing to give of themselves to maintain the relationship. Much can be gained from the union.

SHEEP & HORSE mutual interests
Horses are creative and Sheep are artistic. Together they can create beautiful things. Sheep need to be content with less emotional support from Horses to keep the union happy.

SHEEP & MONKEY supportive
Monkeys can nurture Sheep's involvement in life and keep their spirits up in hard times. Sheep can appreciate Monkeys' cheekiness and indirectly curb their pranks.

SHEEP & SNAKE platonically cultured
Snakes and Sheep, with similar interests, suit each other well as friends. However, Sheep are too sensitive for the usually detached Snakes and will not feel comfortable in an intimate relationship.

SHEEP & TIGER sexually fuelled
These two only have their sex drive in common. In the bedroom they will please each other immensely. Elsewhere, no rapport or respect.

SHEEP & SHEEP devoid of responsibility
Sheep together are harmonious but not usually productive. They will avoid giving advice in case they appear too overbearing.

Negative pairing

SHEEP & RAT lacks long-term interest
Initial attraction possible, but Sheep are too indulgent for work-oriented Rats. Sheep value freedom, creativity and love and Rats value hard work, possessions and financial security.

SHEEP & DRAGON opposing desires
Little will mutually attract or inspire the other in this pairing. Dragons are focused on the big picture and goal accomplishment, Sheep are interested only in living for the moment.

SHEEP & ROOSTER demanding
Little rapport here. Roosters want a more active and socially engaging companion and Sheep will be quite sensitive to Roosters' demands.

SHEEP & OX opposing values
Sheep are too emotional and sensitive for logical and forthright Oxen. Sheep are too easily influenced into indulgences, which principled Oxen frown upon. No respect likely.

Making Friends with a Monkey

Life Roles

FRIEND

Monkeys are extroverts, and will want to socialize frequently with their friends. This can take up a lot of time, as Monkeys love acquiring new friends and are constantly meeting up with different types of people from all walks of life. Monkeys hate being on their own for too long. They enjoy entertainment with their friends, who never find them boring to be around.

RELATIVE

Monkeys will only commit when they are assured they can still have a fun, socially active lifestyle. Few Monkeys do well bogged down with routine, convention and family chores. Their homes are full of activity, littered by toys, games and books. Relatives and other visitors are always welcome, and cherished for the variety they bring. As children, Monkeys are quite mischievous, and will need a good role model to direct their mental dexterity toward worthwhile pursuits.

LOVER

(Those born in a Monkey year and/or during the month of August.) Monkeys make fun and lively lovers. Morals in the bedroom are not their strong suit. Anything goes for Monkeys — provided that it interests them. As they love a challenge, Monkeys are not above competing for the affections of those they desire.

WORKER

Best career choices: comedian, entertainer, actor, traveler, photographer, social columnist. Monkeys are gamblers, renowned for being in volatile financial circumstances. Yet, no matter how much they lose, Monkeys never seem to lose their passion for risk taking. As such they are great as entrepreneurs. At their best, Monkeys are skilled organizers and planners, careful with details.

PERSONAL NEEDS

Monkeys need constant variety and mental stimulation. They need to be shown appreciation for their wit and charm.

Relationships

Positive pairing

MONKEY & RAT mentally engaging

Each admires the other's mental dexterity and artful communication style. They can accomplish much together and address each other's needs for support and understanding.

MONKEY & DRAGON inventive & lively

Drawn to each other — Dragons to Monkeys for their social flair and innovation, and Monkeys to Dragons for their charisma and confidence. Dragons will rule, Monkeys will toe the line. A successful relationship.

MONKEY & SNAKE ingenuity abounds

Pairing of the most intelligent signs, sure to breed ingenuity and innovation. Particularly useful as a business relationship. Snakes and Monkeys can predict future trends and take well-calculated risks.

MONKEY & HORSE energetic flexibility

Monkeys like Horses' enthusiasm and talkative nature, and Horses likes Monkeys' wit and fun approach. However, Horses can be naive and gullible, and Monkeys will find taking advantage irresistible.

MONKEY & SHEEP supportive

Monkeys can nurture Sheep's involvement in life and keep their spirits up in hard times. Sheep can appreciate Monkeys' cheekiness and indirectly curb their pranks.

MONKEY & ROOSTER colorful & witty

A colorful match. Both excel socially and support each other's goals. Monkey will appreciate Rooster's flamboyance, and Rooster Monkey's wit and conversation.

MONKEY & OX lacks sufficient trust

Oxen are usually quick to admire Monkeys' devilish manner, which Monkeys will reward with a little attention. Attraction between them is usually only superficial.

MONKEY & MONKEY rivalry abounds

Constantly teasing and challenging each other; a competitive pairing. Unless at least one has matured, they can get into too much trouble together.

Negative pairing

MONKEY & HARE civil to a point

Will appreciate each other's intelligence and social wit, but have opposing values. Hares seek to blend with others, Monkeys to stand apart.

MONKEY & DOG differences divide

Dogs will like Monkeys' wit and intelligence but soon find them without honor or morals. Monkeys will manipulate Dogs' sense of fair play. Not beneficial, especially for Dogs.

MONKEY & PIG one-sided

Pigs are greatly entertained by Monkeys' antics, while Monkeys enjoy Pigs' sense of fun. However, the relationship will end when Pigs realize they are always on the receiving end.

MONKEY & TIGER traps abound

Monkeys have the most delightful prey in impetuous Tigers, and will draw Tigers into danger too often. Tigers encourage the worst in Monkeys' behavior.

Running Things with a Rooster

Life Roles

FRIEND

Roosters love company, and will frequently entertain. They have a vast array of friends and acquaintances, who admire the lengths Roosters go to in order to impress them. Their homes are highly decorative, immaculately clean and probably too big for their needs. Sensitive to the opinions of others, Roosters constantly seek feedback from their most trusted friends, and can place too much value on their judgments.

RELATIVE

Living with a Rooster can be hard work, as they want their family members to shine in every situation. They set high standards for themselves, their partners, and their children, who can fall short of the mark. Roosters will also go into great debt to finance what they consider just the right home. They can be very direct, but are also protective and generous with loved ones, and will give freely of their time to support them.

LOVER

(Those born in a Rooster year and/or during the month of September.) Roosters like control when it comes to their love life. They like to be showered with praise to feed their secret insecurities. They are renowned as skilled lovers with stamina. Focused on their own performance, Roosters come across as a little self-obsessed to their lovers. In an attempt to win approval, they can be very generous and romantic, even if it means overcommitting on the credit card.

WORKER

Best career choices: presenter, military officer, graphic designer, critic, lecturer/professor. Roosters love tradition, pomp and ceremony, and will be attracted to any occupation in uniform — particularly if they can be adorned with medals and awards. As they are so focused on outward appearances, they will be impressed by titles and high ranks. Yet they have natural talents that often go unnoticed, such as a love of hard work and skill with complexity and detail.

PERSONAL NEEDS

Roosters need a special place in their homes to relax and collect their wits, and also the understanding of their family members when they are too brash.

Relationships

Positive pairing

ROOSTER & OX harmonious
Socially oriented Roosters do not have to
compete for the limelight, and Oxen can
concentrate on the more serious areas of life.

ROOSTER & SNAKE perfect complements
Snakes admire Roosters' extravagance, colorful
appearance and intelligent conversation.
Roosters are smart enough to appreciate
Snakes' wisdom and follow the counsel offered.

ROOSTER & MONKEY colorful & witty
A colorful match. Both excel socially and
support each other's goals. Monkeys will
appreciate Roosters' flamboyance, and Roosters
Monkeys' wit and conversation.

ROOSTER & PIG mutually beneficial
Pigs do not mind if Roosters want to preen and
take control. Pigs just want to be entertained
and provided for. A harmonious relationship.

ROOSTER & TIGER initially captivating
Drawn together instantly as they appear bold
and entertaining to each other. Unfortunately
Roosters will demand perfection, which reckless
Tigers cannot deliver. Tigers can find Roosters
suffocating.

ROOSTER & DRAGON superficial
Both are colorful, hence initial attraction is
guaranteed. However, both can be too self-
obsessed to give what is required for building
and sustaining a committed relationship.

ROOSTER & ROOSTER colorful
Extremely flamboyant relationship. Both will
want to take the lead, and without restraint the
relationship will collapse into disagreements.

ROOSTER & HORSE socially active
An entertaining pair, exuberant and attracted to
the social set. At some stage, Roosters' need for
structure will try to dominate, and then Horses
will run.

Negative pairing

ROOSTER & RAT heated debates ensue
No attraction likely. Rats do not care for
Roosters' flamboyance and bluntness. Roosters
get bored with Rats' pristine presentation and
conformist behavior.

ROOSTER & SHEEP demanding
Little rapport between them. Roosters want a
more active and socially engaging companion
and Sheep will feel upset that they do not meet
Roosters' demands.

ROOSTER & DOG little in common
Each will be too hard on the other. Their strong
convictions will clash and they will not hesitate
to let the other know they are wrong.

ROOSTER & HARE total misunderstanding
Roosters are frank, regardless of the
consequences. Hares will keep their opinions to
themselves for peace. Hares will find Roosters
intolerable, Roosters find Hares insincere.

The Devotion of Dogs

Life Roles

FRIEND

Dogs are friendly and straightforward with friends. As they can be a little suspicious of strangers, they will tend to hold back before making conversation. This serves them well, as they can be so generous that some less reputable types can take advantage of them. However, good-natured Dogs are very popular, and like to have a strong support group of friends around them. They are not the type to be left alone for long.

RELATIVE

Dogs are dependable when it comes to their families, and their children will delight in their playful company. They take their family responsibilities seriously and will be devoted and steadfast in their loyalty. As Dogs are so patient and ready to give in their relationships, there will be little friction. They also like taking on the provider role, and will put the needs of relatives ahead of their own. Dogs have a strong sense of charity toward family.

LOVER

(Those born in a Dog year and/or during the month of October.) Dogs are dedicated and loyal lovers. They do not take affairs of the heart lightly, and will take some time to consider whether their attraction for someone is worth it in the long term: dogs are easily hurt and disappointed. Once in a committed relationship they can be affectionate, protective and self-sacrificing — all traits to be admired in a lover. They can become very attached to their partners.

WORKER

Best career choices: charity worker, missionary, lawyer, judge, doctor, police officer, minister of religion. Dogs take great pride in their work and treat their employers and colleagues as extensions of their family unit. Dogs are the type who will stay committed to one organization for decades and be happy to retire with only a gold watch to show for their efforts. Many Dogs will choose a career in law, where they can address their keen sense of injustice.

PERSONAL NEEDS

Dogs need to be rewarded often and told how much their loyalty and devotion is appreciated by the lucky people in their lives.

Relationships

Positive pairing

DOG & TIGER mutual respect
Complete harmony between impetuous Tiger and patient Dog. Mutual respect of the other's values and courage.

DOG & HORSE supportive & loving
Admire each other's physical engagement with life. Likely to form a successful long-term relationship due to their protective and openly affectionate natures.

DOG & OX mutually respectful
Both are traditionalists and highly principled, and respect and admire each other immensely. Will need to take a lighter approach at times to ensure life is not too serious.

DOG & HARE mutual sharing
Tempers will rarely flare. Each will be happy to sacrifice for the other. While harmonious and considerate, the union can lack initiative.

DOG & SHEEP tolerant & beneficial
Both are compassionate, patient and sensitive, and willing to give of themselves to maintain the relationship. Much can be gained from the union.

DOG & RAT mutually respectful
Harmony probable. Rats appreciate Dogs' loyalty and respect their morality. Dogs feel inspired by Rats' ambition. As both are prone to insecurities and self-doubt, the relationship can hit low points.

DOG & DOG congenial compatibility
Understanding and considerate, two Dogs can have a successful union provided they do not take life too seriously and add some adventure to their daily routine.

DOG & PIG mutually beneficial
Light-hearted Pigs can cheer up sometimes depressed Dogs, and Dogs will appreciate Pigs' attention. A happy union, provided Dogs do not stand too much by their principles.

Negative pairing

DOG & SNAKE misunderstood intentions
Snakes will lead and Dogs follow obediently. But secretive Snakes will be too much for upfront Dogs to understand. Snakes will eventually tire of Dogs' moralizing.

DOG & MONKEY differences divide
Dogs will like Monkeys' wit and intelligence but soon find them without honor or morals. Monkeys will manipulate Dogs' sense of fair play. Not beneficial, especially for Dogs.

DOG & DRAGON differences do not impress
Dogs are too serious and judgmental for optimistic, entertaining Dragons, who like breaking the rules. Dragons will be an endless source of misbehavior to frustrate Dogs even further.

DOG & ROOSTER little in common
Each will be too hard on the other. Their strong convictions will clash and they will not hesitate to let the other know they are wrong.

Life's a Party with Pigs

Life Roles

FRIEND
Pigs are the easiest people to get along with in the Chinese zodiac. Their generosity, sincerity and easy-going attitude make them popular. Their genuine concern for others is well appreciated and they will be frequently sought out to lend a sympathetic ear. As they love to indulge in sensual delights, wining, dining and dancing all play an important part in a Pig's cherished lifestyle.

RELATIVE
Home is the preferred place for Pigs. They will not be attracted to adventure and distant places, only to the glow of a warm hearth and the smiles of a loving family. They are natural parents and homemakers and show considerable patience and understanding with their loved ones. The Chinese believe a Pig brings much happiness to a family and hence Pig children are always a welcome addition to a family.

LOVER
(Those born in a Pig year and/or during the month of November.) Pigs are addicted to love and the art of lovemaking. This sign knows how to engage all the senses in wild abandon with no care for the consequences. Pigs' lovemaking is enduring, tender and compassionate. They are openly demonstrative with their partners and will beam in the glow of returned affections. Pig partners will be given a lot of freedom.

WORKER
Best career choices: homemaker, childcare worker, nurse, counselor, chef, artist. Pigs are not usually career- or even work-oriented. They are happy for someone else to be the provider so they can be left at home to nurture. If they must work, they are not too choosy about the occupation — provided the pay is sufficient to meet their needs. Their friendly, easy-going nature will ensure their popularity in the workplace.

PERSONAL NEEDS
Pigs need to be supported financially and emotionally and appreciated for the love and sincerity they bring to a relationship.

Relationships

Positive pairing

PIG & HARE a winning pair

Both are considerate and peace-loving. Together they can create the gentle harmony each requires. From this comfortable base both can succeed in their individual projects.

PIG & SHEEP supportive & creative

Both can provide the comfort and nurturing atmosphere the other needs most. Have a carefree existence together, encouraging and supportive of each other's talents.

PIG & TIGER life's a party

Pigs will rule the home and appreciate Tigers' need to roam the world outside. These two fall naturally into their most cherished roles — homemaker Pigs and provider Tigers.

PIG & DRAGON surprisingly successful

Little in common. However, in a gregarious mood Dragons will sweep awestruck Pigs into the air, and both will be happy with Dragons in command.

PIG & DOG mutually beneficial

Light-hearted Pigs can cheer up sometimes depressed Dogs, and Dogs will appreciate Pigs' attention. A happy union provided Dogs do not stand too much by their principles.

PIG & HORSE socially active & popular

Both like having a good time and will maintain a hectic social life. Provided Pigs do not overly indulge, Horses will stay interested.

PIG & PIG selfish & indulgent

Two Pigs are a delight together and relish each other as they indulge in all kinds of pleasure with abandon. The risk here is overindulgence.

PIG & RAT initially resourceful

While Rats will earn their keep, Pigs will be just as quick to spend it. Rats initially feel appreciated in this breadwinner role, but soon tire of Pigs' indulgences.

PIG & OX initially peaceful

Both require harmonious surroundings to be productive. Both provide peace and quiet, but Pig's self-indulgence and lack of restraint will cause friction.

PIG & ROOSTER mutually beneficial

Pigs don't mind if Roosters wants to preen and take control. Pigs just wants to be entertained and provided for. A harmonious relationship.

Negative pairing

PIG & SNAKE lacking appreciation

Pigs are easy to read, as they hold nothing back and live for the moment. Snakes are hard to read and cautious. A relationship between the two is virtually impossible.

PIG & MONKEY one-sided

Pigs are greatly entertained by Monkeys' antics, while Monkeys enjoy Pigs' sense of fun. However, the relationship can end when Pigs realize they are always on the receiving end.

Meeting Your Match

Rewarding and Challenging Combinations

Each of the twelve animals of Chinese astrology has varying degrees of natural rapport with the other eleven, or of antagonism toward them. While there is always hope for every pairing, the Chinese believe some pairings are far more favorable than others, and that this has a direct influence on each partner's overall success in life. Use the table below to find your most rewarding and challenging combinations. The scale is as follows: 5 = most rewarding, 1 = most challenging.

Combination scale

5 = Perfect: An ideal combination for long-term happiness and success
4 = Rewarding: Mostly a happy and beneficial union
3 = Harmonious: A balancing act — there are both good and unfavorable times
2 = Frustrating: More effort and focused energy are required to make things work
1 = Combative: A tragic case of opposites attracting and causing more pain than gain

	Rat	Ox	Tiger	Hare	Dragon	Snake	Horse	Sheep	Monkey	Rooster	Dog	Pig
Rat	3	4	2	4	⑤	4	❶	2	⑤	2	3	3
Ox	4	3	2	4	2	⑤	2	❶	3	⑤	4	3
Tiger	2	2	3	4	4	2	⑤	3	❶	3	⑤	4
Hare	4	4	4	3	2	3	2	⑤	2	❶	3	⑤
Dragon	⑤	2	4	2	3	4	3	2	⑤	3	❶	4
Snake	4	⑤	2	3	4	3	2	3	4	⑤	2	❶
Horse	❶	2	⑤	2	3	2	3	4	3	3	⑤	4
Sheep	2	❶	3	⑤	2	3	4	3	4	2	4	⑤
Monkey	⑤	3	❶	2	⑤	4	3	4	3	4	2	2
Rooster	2	⑤	3	❶	3	⑤	3	2	4	3	2	4
Dog	3	4	⑤	3	❶	2	⑤	4	2	2	3	4
Pig	3	3	4	⑤	4	❶	4	⑤	2	4	4	3

The Affinity Trios

Achieving harmony with others is a key principle of Chinese astrology. A successful life is achieved through relationships with others that support and enrich rather than oppose. The following groups of three are said to share some personality traits that promote similar values, behavior and outlook on life. Relationships within each group are said to be the most harmonious possible, as a natural and strong rapport is easily achieved.

The Initiators ~ Rat, Monkey, Dragon
Practical, optimistic, action-oriented, self-motivated, innovative, enthusiastic

The Visionaries ~ Ox, Rooster, Snake
Wise, reflective, pragmatic, intellectual, thorough, patient, steadfast

The Defenders ~ Tiger, Dog, Horse
Passionate, independent, selfless, loyal, honest, fair, courageous

The Co-operators ~ Hare, Pig, Sheep
Intuitive, supportive, sensitive, peaceful, sincere, creative, diplomatic

Conflicting Opposites

In keeping with the principle of harmony and balance, each of the twelve animal signs finds their opposite in one other sign. The Chinese believe that relationships between the following opposing signs will generally bring conflict to those involved, and as such are best avoided.

RAT and HORSE
OX and SHEEP
TIGER and MONKEY
HARE and ROOSTER
DRAGON and DOG
SNAKE and PIG

The Value of Astrology

The ancient Chinese placed great importance on astrology, using it as a complex system that could shed some light on individual personalities, and make predictions for people about likely compatibilities before they plunged into business, marriage, friendship and parenthood. The local astrologer was often an esteemed and trusted counselor whose advice was taken seriously.

Chinese astrology reveals an array of unique personality types, with time and date of birth governing them. According to the Chinese, success in life comes from the ability to form useful and productive relationships. This is achieved by the careful balancing of personality traits and energy types.

It is important to note that no personality type is "better" than another. Each of the types described in this book represents a beneficial approach to life. Wisdom is said to be in the hands of those who understand this, and apply appropriate behaviour and flexibility in their communication style.

This book has attempted to guide you towards understanding and interpreting the different signs of the Chinese zodiac and the way they relate to each other. This book has also highlighted the importance of the animal sign which rules the year, month and time of birth, as well as the elements associated with the animals and the year of birth, as they all influence the personality in a particular way.

Glossary of Terms

Ascendant	The animal sign ruling the time of birth
Dominant animal	The animal sign ruling the year of birth
Dominant element	The element ruling the year of birth
Elements	Nature's influence on the signs of the zodiac: Metal, Water, Wood, Fire, Earth
Love sign	The animal sign ruling the month of birth
Natural element	The element normally associated with each animal sign
Pure sign	Occurs when the same animal sign rules both the year and time of birth
Yang energy	Positive/masculine energy, indicating extroversion
Yin energy	Negative/feminine energy, indicating introversion

Reading More about Chinese Astrology

Choy, H. & Henwood, B. (1997), *Feng Shui*, Lansdowne Publishing, Sydney.

Craze, R. (1998), *The Chinese Astrology Handbook*, Lorenz Books, London.

Giles, B. & The Diagram Group (1996), *Collins Gem Chinese Astrology*, HarperCollins, Glasgow.

Kwok, Man-Ho (1987), *Authentic Chinese Horoscopes*, Arrow Books Ltd, London.

Lau, K. (1994), *Secrets of Chinese Astrology*, Tenyu Books, New York.

Lau, T. (1995), *The Chinese Horoscopes Guide to Relationships*, Souvenir Press Ltd, London.

Lau, T. (1995), *The Handbook of Chinese Horoscopes*, 3rd edn, Souvenir Press Ltd, London.

Luxon, B. (1998), *Chinese Astrology*, Greenwich Editions, London.

Somerville, N. (1997), *Your Chinese Horoscope 1998*, Thorsons, London

Too, L. (1996), *Chinese Astrology For Romance & Relationships*, Konsep Books, Malaysia.

Walters, D. (1994), *Chinese Love Signs*, S. Abdul Majeed & Co, Malaysia.

White S. (1987), *The New Astrology*, Pan Books, London.

White, S. (1994), *The New Chinese Astrology*, Pan Books, London.

List of Years and Astrology Signs 1900–2019

Lunar Year	Date From	Date To	Dominant Animal	Dominant Element	Lunar Year	Date From	Date To	Dominant Animal	Dominant Element
1900	31/3/00	18/2/01	Rat	Metal	1929	10/2/29	29/1/30	Snake	Earth
1901	19/2/01	7/2/02	Ox	Metal	1930	30/1/30	16/2/31	Horse	Metal
1902	8/2/02	28/1/03	Tiger	Water	1931	17/2/31	5/2/32	Sheep	Metal
1903	29/1/03	15/2/04	Hare	Water	1932	6/2/32	25/1/33	Monkey	Water
1904	16/2/04	3/2/05	Dragon	Wood	1933	26/1/33	13/2/34	Rooster	Water
1905	4/2/05	24/1/06	Snake	Wood	1934	14/2/34	3/2/35	Dog	Wood
1906	25/1/06	12/2/07	Horse	Fire	1935	4/2/35	23/1/36	Pig	Wood
1907	13/2/07	1/2/08	Sheep	Fire	1936	24/1/36	10/2/37	Rat	Fire
1908	2/2/08	21/1/09	Monkey	Earth	1937	11/2/37	30/1/38	Ox	Fire
1909	22/1/09	9/2/10	Rooster	Earth	1938	31/1/38	18/2/39	Tiger	Earth
1910	10/2/10	29/1/11	Dog	Metal	1939	19/2/39	7/2/40	Hare	Earth
1911	30/1/11	17/2/12	Pig	Metal	1940	8/2/40	26/1/41	Dragon	Metal
1912	18/2/12	5/2/13	Rat	Water	1941	27/1/41	14/2/42	Snake	Metal
1913	6/2/13	25/1/14	Ox	Water	1942	15/2/42	4/2/43	Horse	Water
1914	26/1/14	13/2/15	Tiger	Wood	1943	5/2/43	24/1/44	Sheep	Water
1915	14/2/15	2/2/16	Hare	Wood	1944	25/1/44	12/2/45	Monkey	Wood
1916	3/2/16	22/1/17	Dragon	Fire	1945	13/2/45	1/2/46	Rooster	Wood
1917	23/1/17	10/2/18	Snake	Fire	1946	2/2/46	21/1/47	Dog	Fire
1918	11/2/18	31/1/19	Horse	Earth	1947	22/1/47	9/2/48	Pig	Fire
1919	1/2/19	19/2/20	Sheep	Earth	1948	10/2/48	28/1/49	Rat	Earth
1920	20/2/20	7/2/21	Monkey	Metal	1949	29/1/49	16/2/50	Ox	Earth
1921	8/2/21	27/1/22	Rooster	Metal	1950	17/2/50	5/2/51	Tiger	Metal
1922	28/1/22	15/2/23	Dog	Water	1951	6/2/51	26/1/52	Hare	Metal
1923	16/2/23	4/2/24	Pig	Water	1952	27/1/52	13/2/53	Dragon	Water
1924	5/2/24	24/1/25	Rat	Wood	1953	14/2/53	2/2/54	Snake	Water
1925	25/1/25	12/2/26	Ox	Wood	1954	3/2/54	23/1/55	Horse	Wood
1926	13/2/26	1/2/27	Tiger	Fire	1955	24/1/55	11/2/56	Sheep	Wood
1927	2/2/27	22/1/28	Hare	Fire	1956	12/2/56	30/1/57	Monkey	Fire
1928	23/1/28	9/2/29	Dragon	Earth	1957	31/1/57	17/2/58	Rooster	Fire

Lunar Year	Date From	Date To	Dominant Animal	Dominant Element	Lunar Year	Date From	Date To	Dominant Animal	Dominant Element
1958	18/2/58	7/2/59	Dog	Earth	1989	6/2/89	26/1/90	Snake	Earth
1959	8/2/59	27/1/60	Pig	Earth	1990	27/1/90	14/2/91	Horse	Metal
1960	28/1/60	14/2/61	Rat	Metal	1991	15/2/91	3/2/92	Sheep	Metal
1961	15/2/61	4/2/62	Ox	Metal	1992	4/2/92	22/1/93	Monkey	Water
1962	5/2/62	24/1/63	Tiger	Water	1993	23/1/93	9/2/94	Rooster	Water
1963	25/1/63	12/2/64	Hare	Water	1994	10/2/94	30/1/95	Dog	Wood
1964	13/2/64	1/2/65	Dragon	Wood	1995	31/1/95	18/2/96	Pig	Wood
1965	2/2/65	20/1/66	Snake	Wood	1996	19/2/96	6/2/97	Rat	Fire
1966	21/1/66	8/2/67	Horse	Fire	1997	7/2/97	27/1/98	Ox	Fire
1967	9/2/67	29/1/68	Sheep	Fire	1998	28/1/98	15/2/99	Tiger	Earth
1968	30/1/68	16/2/69	Monkey	Earth	1999	16/2/99	4/2/2000	Hare	Earth
1969	17/2/69	5/2/70	Rooster	Earth	2000	5/2/2000	23/1/2001	Dragon	Metal
1970	6/2/70	26/1/71	Dog	Metal	2001	24/1/01	11/2/2002	Snake	Metal
1971	27/1/71	15/1/72	Pig	Metal	2002	12/2/02	31/1/2003	Horse	Water
1972	16/1/72	2/2/73	Rat	Water	2003	1/2/03	21/1/2004	Sheep	Water
1973	3/2/73	22/1/74	Ox	Water	2004	22/1/04	8/2/2005	Monkey	Wood
1974	23/1/74	10/2/75	Tiger	Wood	2005	9/2/05	28/1/2006	Rooster	Wood
1975	11/2/75	30/1/76	Hare	Wood	2006	29/1/06	17/2/2007	Dog	Fire
1976	31/1/76	17/2/77	Dragon	Fire	2007	18/2/07	6/2/2008	Pig	Fire
1977	18/2/77	6/2/78	Snake	Fire	2008	7/2/08	25/1/2009	Rat	Earth
1978	7/2/78	27/1/79	Horse	Earth	2009	26/1/09	13/2/2010	Ox	Earth
1979	28/1/79	15/2/80	Sheep	Earth	2010	14/2/10	2/2/2011	Tiger	Metal
1980	16/2/80	4/2/81	Monkey	Metal	2011	3/2/11	22/1/2012	Hare	Metal
1981	5/2/81	24/1/82	Rooster	Metal	2012	23/1/12	9/2/2013	Dragon	Water
1982	25/1/82	12/2/83	Dog	Water	2013	10/2/13	30/1/2014	Snake	Water
1983	13/2/83	1/2/84	Pig	Water	2014	31/1/14	18/2/2015	Horse	Wood
1984*	2/2/84	19/2/85	Rat	Wood	2015	19/2/15	7/2/2016	Sheep	Wood
1985	20/2/85	8/2/86	Ox	Wood	2016	8/2/16	27/1/2017	Monkey	Fire
1986	9/2/86	28/1/87	Tiger	Fire	2017	28/1/17	15/2/2018	Rooster	Fire
1987	29/1/87	16/2/88	Hare	Fire	2018	16/2/18	4/2/2019	Dog	Earth
1988	17/2/88	5/2/89	Dragon	Earth	2019	5/2/19	24/1/2020	Pig	Earth

* The year 1984 is the first year of the newest Chinese 60-year life cycle.

The Law of Least Effort

Nature's intelligence functions with effortless ease — with carefreeness, harmony, and love.
And when we harness the forces of harmony, joy, and love, we create success and good fortune with effortless ease.

Deepak Chopra — The Seven Spiritual Laws of Success

This edition published by Barnes & Noble, Inc.,
by arrangement with Lansdowne Publishing

2001 Barnes & Noble Books
Reprinted 2001

ISBN 0-7607-2360-5

M 10 9 8 7 6 5 4 3 2

Text: D J Burns
Designer: Avril Makula
Editor: Avril Janks
Illustrator: Sue Ninham
Project Co-ordinator: Kate Merrifield
Set in Revival on QuarkXPress
Printed in Singapore by Tien Wah Press (Pte) Ltd